AMPHIBIANS

INTRODUCTION

John Coborn

People have always kept pets of one kind or another, and during the last few decades we have seen a remarkable increase in the number of hobbyists who want to keep frogs, toads, salamanders, and newts instead of (or in addition to) the more conventional cats, dogs, rabbits, and canaries.

What is it that makes many of us want us to keep such unusual pets? Perhaps it is the isolation of many of us from the great natural world. Many who live in towns and cities have only the occasional opportunity to experience the natural environment. But by keeping a small parcel of nature in the home, we compensate for what we would otherwise never get to see. Another reason is that there still is a whole lot we don't know about amphibians, and the quest for more knowledge is never satisfied.

Another very important factor is that many animals, amphibians included, are in serious decline in their natural habitats, especially those close to urban areas. We are very aware of some of the reasons for this, and most seem to be our (humankind's) fault. Development not only wipes out many amphibian habitats but also increases the amount of pollution. Fertilizers, insecticides, and herbicides are spayed in our gardens and farms, then rain and irrigation wash the toxic residue into ponds, creeks, and rivers, making life difficult for many aquatic creatures. Most amphibians are unable to cope with radical chemical changes in their environment, so their numbers continue to decrease.

You can do some things to help the native amphibians in your area. For example, you can construct garden ponds, which provide plenty of vegetative cover, and eschew the use of harmful checmicals. In many cases there are good organic alternatives to chemical sprays.

The home amphibian hobbyist can also help in a small but significant way by taking good care of his or her pets and encouraging them to breed. Many species may someday exist only in captivity (that already has happened to a few), so captive-bred specimens may be the only survivors of a once-widespread race. Scary stuff, but reality nevertheless.

This book was written for the prospective amphibian keeper who wishes to find out all he or she can about the fascinating hobby of amphibian-keeping. Included is material that hopefully will be of interest to all people who have a concern for nature in general.

© T.F.H. Publications, Inc.

Distributed in the UNITED STATES to the Pet Trade by T.F.H. Publications, Inc., 1 TFH Plaza, Neptune City, NJ 07753; on the Internet at www.tfh.com; in CANADA by Rolf C. Hagen Inc., 3225 Sartelon St., Montreal, Quebec H4R 1E8; Pet Trade by H & L Pet Supplies Inc., 27 Kingston Crescent, Kitchener, Ontario N2B 2T6; in ENGLAND by T.F.H. Publications, PO Box 74, Havant PO9 5TT; in AUSTRALIA AND THE SOUTH PACIFIC by T.F.H. (Australia), Pty. Ltd., Box 149, Brookvale 2100 N.S.W., Australia; in NEW ZEALAND by Brooklands Aquarium Ltd., 5 McGiven Drive, New Plymouth, RD1 New Zealand; in SOUTH AFRICA by Rolf C. Hagen S.A. (PTY.) LTD., P.O. Box 201199, Durban North 4016, South Africa; in JAPAN by T.F.H. Publications. Published by T.F.H. Publications, Inc.

MANUFACTURED IN THE
UNITED STATES OF AMERICA
BY T.F.H. PUBLICATIONS, INC.

CONTENTS

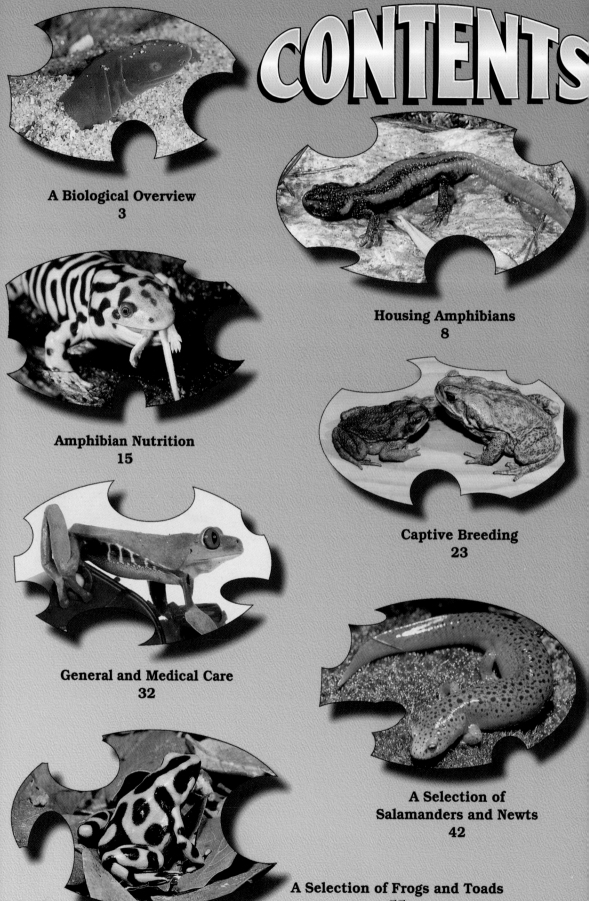

A BIOLOGICAL OVERVIEW

During the late Devonian period, about 350 million years ago, an amazing thing happened, something that forever changed life on this earth.

Certain lobe-finned fishes had been exploiting the changes in their aquatic environment by developing the ability to exist with relatively small amounts of water. Their fins developed into flippers whereby they could move from one shallow pool to the next, and they developed various means of respiration through the skin and through primitive lungs.

As they gradually became more adapted to life on land, they left their fishy life behind and became amphibians. They were the first vertebrates to spend lengthy periods away from the water. Without this giant evolutionary step, the reptiles, the birds, and the mammals may have never become the creatures that we know today.

Many of those early amphibians were relatively enormous when compared with their modern descendants, and like the dinosaurs, they eventually became extinct. Considerable fossil material from these large amphibians, as well as some smaller ones, has been found, however, and we are able to form a picture of how some of them may have looked. One of the largest, *Mastadonsaurus*, had a huge crocodile-like head mounted on a salamander-like body. It was 4 m/13 ft long! For a very long time (about

GEOLOGIC TIME SCALE

Era	Period	Epoch	Approximate number of years ago (millions of years)
Cenozoic	Quaternary	Holocene	10,000 years ago to the present
		Pleistocene	2
	Tertiary	Pliocene	13
		Miocene	25
		Oligocene	36
		Eocene	58
		Paleocene	65
Mesozoic	Cretaceous		136
	Jurassic		190
	Triassic		225
Paleozoic	Permian		280
	Carboniferous		345
AMPHIBIANS BEGAN TO EVOLVE	Devonian		405
	Silurian		425
	Ordovician		500
	Cambrian		600
Precambrian			3,980

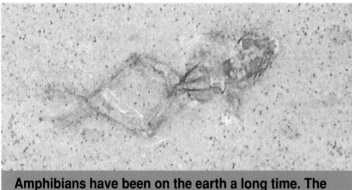

Amphibians have been on the earth a long time. The earliest known amphibian fossils are from the late Triassic and Jurassic periods, between 170 and 200 million years ago. Photo by J. Kellner.

them a most fascinating group of animals to study.

The word 'amphibian' is derived from the Greek *amphibios*, which means 'having a double life.' This refers to the general idea that amphibians spend their lives alternately in water and on land. Most amphibians require water in which to reproduce. Some are very dependent on water for everything else as well, but a few have mastered life on land.

The class Amphibia is divided into three orders—Anura (frogs and toads), Caudata (salamanders and newts), and Gymnophiona (caecilians).

100 million years), thousands of species of all sizes were the dominant class of animals upon the earth.

Unfortunately, we have not yet found any direct fossil evidence to link these pioneer land-dwellers to the contemporary amphibians, and we can only speculate about how our modern frogs and salamanders evolved from the earlier forms. The oldest known fossil evidence of our modern amphibians is from the late Triassic and the Jurassic periods, making them between 170 and 200 million years old.

The amphibians form today's smallest vertebrate class, and, with about 4,000 species, they comprise just 10% of the total living vertebrate fauna. In spite of this, the amphibians display an amazing variety of form, color, and habit, making

Frogs and Toads

These form the order Anura (meaning 'tail-less') and comprise around 20 families, about 300 genera, and over 4000 different species, making them the most numerous and varied group of amphibians. They are found on every continent except Antarctica and occupy habitats in tropical, subtropical, and temperate areas. There are terrestrial, burrowing, arboreal, and aquatic amphibians, and

This particular frog fossil (plus the one pictured above) was found in the Santana formation and reported in 1988. It is believed the animal depicted was approaching adulthood when it died. Photo by J. Kellner.

All frogs and toads belong to the order Anura. Anura is one of three orders in the class Amphibia. Photo of the European Grass Toad, *Bufo viridis*, by K. H. Switak.

At present, there are around 20 frog and toad families. Shown is a Harlequin Frog, *Atelopus varius*, which belongs in the family Bufonidae. Photo by K. H. Switak.

Frogs and toads can be found in a wide variety of habitats and on every continent except Antarctica. Photo of a Southern Cricket Frog, *Acris gryllus*, by W. P. Mara.

their habitats range from tropical to temperate forests, deserts to grasslands, and plains to mountain peaks. Put simply, they're everywhere!

What, might you ask, is the difference between a frog and a toad? There is no real scientific

Some anurans live in the water, others live on land, and then there are those that live in trees and bushes. Many of the latter are called treefrogs, such as this beautiful Red-eyed Treefrog, *Agalychnis callidryas*. Photo by Isabelle Francais.

explanation, but 'frog' is normally applied to those anurans with a moist, slippery skin, while 'toad' refers to those with with a dry, 'warty' skin. Many of the latter belong to the genus *Bufo*, known, unsurprisingly, as the 'true toads.' For convenience, we will refer to all frogs and toads

collectively as anurans except when talking about particular species.

Everyone knows what a typical anuran looks like. It has a squat body, long hindlimbs, and almost always lacks a tail (except in the case of recently metamorphosed specimens and the very

few species that actually retain some tail). Its broad head and thick neck are not very distinct from the body, and it has a very wide mouth. Most species have a long sticky tongue with which to catch their prey (mainly insects), but there are some exceptions. Most anurans have some webbing between the toes to assist with swimming, while many treefrogs in particular have adhesive digital pads to help them climb about on many surfaces that would be off-limits to other anurans.

Salamanders and Newts

These form the order Caudata (meaning 'tailed') and comprise nine families, about 60 genera, and some 360 species. The family is confined to North and South America, Europe, North Africa, and Asia. Only in South America are there species south of the equator. Caudates have not expanded their range to the extent of frogs and toads, and most stay close to permanent water although there still are a few terrestrial, burrowing, and aquatic forms. A handful of species even are semiarboreal.

The difference between a

Salamanders and newts are classified in the family Caudata, which contains nine families and about sixty genera. Photo of a 'Red Eft' (*Notophthalmus viridescens*) by Paul Freed.

newt and a salamander, like that of frog and toad, is colloquial rather than scientific. The word 'newt' is usually reserved for those species that become almost totally aquatic

during the breeding season in the spring and take on a nuptial courtship dress then return to land when the breeding season is over.

A typical salamander has an elongate body, a tail often as long as head and body combined, four limbs of similar size (though there are some exceptions) and, usually, a head set off quite distinctly from the body. Some salamanders have a long sticky tongue for catching prey.

Caecilians

These form the order Gymnophiona (meaning 'limbless') and comprise six families, around 33 genera, and some 160 species. They occur in the tropics of Central and South America, Africa, and Asia. They are the least-studied of the amphibians. They are limbless, wormlike, burrowing or

There are a handful of semiarboreal salamanders (most are terrestrial or aquatic). One of the more attractive forms is the Nauta Mushroom-tongued Salamander, *Bolitoglossa altamazonica*. Photo by R. T. Zappalorti.

aquatic, and have rudimentary eyes. Species range in length from 3 in/7 cm to 4 ft/120 cm. Many people mistake them for eels (aquatic varieties) or snakes (terrestrial varieties).

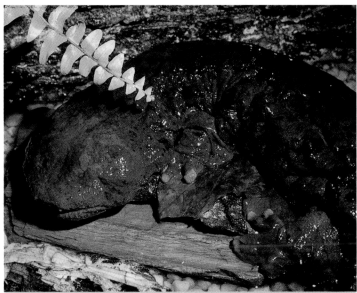

Most salamanders are considered relatively small, but some can attain a length of up to 18 in/45.7 cm or more. This Ozark Hellbender, *Cryptobranchus alleganiensis bishopi*, for example, can reach a maximum length of around 22 in/55.8 cm. Photo by K. T. Nemuras.

Caecilians make up the order Gymnophiona and occur in tropical America, Africa, and Asia. Photo of a Rio Cauca Caecilian, *Typhlonectes natans*, by M. P. and C. Piednoir.

Caecilians, like most amphibians, need to stay moist. Thus, it should come as no surprise that they are most commonly found in areas of abundant rainfall. Photo of a Mexican Caecilian, *Dermophis mexicana*, by R. D. Bartlett.

Caecilians probably are the least-studied of the amphibians. Photo of a Koh Tao Island Caecilian, *Ichthyophis kohtaoensis*, by K. T. Nemuras.

HOUSING AMPHIBIANS

In view of the great variety of amphibians and their natural habitats, it is obvious that there is a wide range of enclosures and setups to choose from. As most amphibians require a moist environment, glass seems to be the best choice for cage material.

There is an increasing number of commercially made cages specially devised for keeping amphibians and reptiles, so it would be to your benefit to become familiar with what is available. However, the hobbyist who wants to breed his or her stock will probably have to improvise at certain times. All kinds of containers can be made suitable for raising tadpoles, young frogs, and young salamanders. Large plastic food-storage containers are ideal for many species.

Cages for captive amphibians can be placed in three different categories, these being based on the basic natural habitat of the inmates. Aquatic species

The best type of enclosure to use when housing amphibians is one made of glass. Glass tolerates moisture better than wood, and moisture is essential to an amphibian's health. Photo by Mark Staniszewski.

(such as those of the genera *Pipa, Xenopus, Hymenochirus,* and *Amphiuma,* for example) will be kept in an aquatic setup. Semiaquatic species (many ranid frogs, newts, and some salamanders, for example) will require an aquaterrarium with a substantial pool plus a generous land area. Terrestrial amphibians, (some frogs and toads plus some salamanders) will require a terrarium with only a small water

It is vital that you learn about your pet's natural habitat before setting up its enclosure. If you arrange the enclosure incorrectly, the animal could die in a relatively short time. This Pink-headed Dwarf Caecilian, *Microcaecilia albiceps,* for example, lives in moist terrestrial situations. Photo by Paul Freed.

When setting up and amphibian's captive home, the main idea is to create a world that is reflective of the one the animal lived in previously. Photo of a montane tropical rainforest (cloud forest) in Guatemala by Zoltan Takacs.

should be thoroughly rinsed through before use. The gravel layer should be about 2 in/5 cm deep at the front and 3 in/7.5 cm at the rear. This will allow debris to collect at the front, allowing it to be easily siphoned out. If your filtration system is in the rear, then reverse the arrangement, making the substrate layer slightly higher in the front.

Decorations can include rocks and bogwood. All rocks should be thoroughly scrubbed before use,

supply, but it will still be necessary to maintain a moist environment.

The Aquarium

Most modern aquarium tanks are made of glass panels held together with silicon sealant. Most hobbyists like to set up their tanks with a natural-looking landscape. Such decorative accommodations can become a main feature in the lounge or den.

The first consideration is the substrate. Aquarium gravel is the most popular choice, and rightly so. Sand or soil will soon get churned up and cloud the water. Newly purchased gravel

Kakadu National Park, in Australia, at the end of the dry season. This locality is home to a number of amphibians, including Rust-eyed Treefrog, *Litoria rothi*. Photo by K. H. Switak.

A lowland tropical rainforest in Indonesia. Photo by Zoltan Takacs.

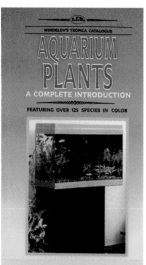

To learn more about plants that can be used in setups for aquatic amphibians, get a copy of TFH's *Aquarium Plants, A Complete Introduction* (CO-002S) by Holger Windelov.

(mudpuppies, amphiumas, etc.), as they will be continually grubbed out. Use sturdy plants and try to get them established before you include the animals. For more information on cultivating water plants in aquaria, you are advised to refer to the excellent little book *Aquarium Plants, a Complete Introduction* written by Holger Windelov and published by T.F.H Publications.

The water quality in the aquarium is important. Like many

Greenhouses and other types of outdoor enclosures are becoming more and more popular with serious hobbyists. If you have some backyard space to spare, you should try setting up something like this. Photo by Mark Staniszewski.

and, due to the possibility of alkaline leach, limestone should not be used at all. Bogwood can be obtained from aquarists suppliers. Do not use freshly cut wood as it may leach toxic substances.

Aquarium plants can make or break the beauty of your setup. Plants often are as difficult or more difficult to keep alive as the amphibians. It is a waste of time using plants with very large aquatic amphibians species of fish, most amphibians cannot tolerate treated domestic water. So, whenever possible, rainwater or strained pond/river water should be used. If there is no alternative to domestic water, this should be allowed to stand in a separate container for a few days before use. This will allow the water "age" and any chlorine to dissipate.

It is advised that you have a filtration system in your aquarium tank as aquatic amphibians can soon pollute the

Tropical aquatic species, such as this *Hymenochiurus*, will require a heated water body. A fully submersible heater works best for this task. Photo by U. E. Friese.

Providing captive amphibians with the correct photoperiod (day/night cycle) is very important. Photoperiod often is a factor in determining an amphibian's behaviorisms. Bulbs designed specifically for the keeping of herptiles now are available at many pet shops. Photo courtesy of Energy Savers.

Along with proper lighting and heating, fully aquatic amphibians need an efficient filtration system. Without one, their keeper may end up performing water changes every day or so. Photo of an African Clawed Frog, *Xenopus laevis*, by Mark Smith.

water. You can use undergravel filters or box filters powered by an aerator. The aerator will also help keep the water sweet and fresh. For more efficient filtration, use a submersible or external power filter. Your aquarist supplier will be able to show you a

Gravel probably is the most commonly used substrate in the keeping of aquatic amphibians. Photo of a Surinam Toad, *Pipa pipa*, by W. P. Mara.

range of filter models.

Some tropical species (*Xenopus, Hymenochirus,* and *Pipa*, for example) will require that the water be heated somewhat. An ordinary thermostatically controlled aquarium heater set at about 77°F/25°C will be ideal for this purpose.

A full-spectrum light will be beneficial to both the animals and plants

Most anurans can be put in an aquaterrarium setup, i.e., one that is arranged with more or less equal bodies of land and water. A simple way to set one up is by dividing a glass tank with the aid of some sealant and a sheet of plastic or glass. Photo of a Malayan Leopard Frog, *Rana signata*, by Paul Freed.

In aquaterrarium setups, you may find that certain amphibian species spend more time in one section of the enclosure than the other. Photo of a Bullfrog, *Rana catesbeiana*, by Aaron Norman.

in your aquarium. It should be turned off at night. Also, it is advised that you provide seasonal changes in photoperiod based on that which is natural in the habitat of the species being kept, especially if breeding is planned.

The Aquaterrarium

This is basically an aquarium supplied with an area of land so that semi-aquatic amphibians can enter and leave the water as they wish. The simplest aquaterrarium is a fish tank with a glass divider about 6 in/15 cm high held with silicon sealant and laid in at a sloping angle. One side can be filled up with gravel, into which potted plants are sunk. You also can decorate with rocks and moss, which will provide a few hiding places for the inmates.

The other side of the partition is filled with a shallow gravel substrate and then with water. A few rocks arranged next to the partition will allow your pets to enter and leave the water easily. The water area can otherwise be set up just like the aquarium, with a few aquatic plants and a filter. An aquarium aerator used in the water will help keep the water sweet and will contribute to the humidity of the environment.

And although most amphibian cages must be kept quite humid, we must not forget the importance of ventilation. A badly ventilated terrarium will harbor stagnant air, allowing for the proliferation of various unpleasant organisms. You will have to strike a

balance between the humidity and the ventilation. Terrarium lids must always have ventilation grids. If you are using a simple sheet of glass as a lid, make sure it is propped up just slightly to allow for the free exchange of air. (Be careful not to make the space so wide that some of your amphibians could escape—some amphibians can squeeze through the narrowest spaces.)

The Terrarium

The terrarium is a cage in which there is no large area of water. Again, you can use an ordinary aquarium tank

Ventilation is an important housing consideration that many keepers overlook. All amphibians will suffer if left in enclosures that harbor stagnant air. Photo of a Kweichow Crocodile Newt, *Tylototriton kweichowensis*, by Aaron Norman.

Most amphibians require plenty of moisture. One easy way to provide this to captive specimens is by spray-misting the inside of the enclosure every day or so. Most species also won't mind having their bodies sprayed as well. Photo of a Vienna Newt, *Triturus carnifex*, by Mark Staniszewski.

The Golden Mantella Frog, *Mantella aurantiaca*; a popular yet delicate species that requires a great deal of bodily moisture. Photo by W. P. Mara.

Some keepers prefer to surpass the 'daily misting' method of providing moisture in an enclosure and go right to the more technical approach of placing an airstone (which is attached to an air pump via plastic aquarium tubing) in a bowl of warm water. Photo of a pair of Golfodulcean Poison Frogs, *Phyllobates vittatus*, by K. H. Switak.

to set up a terrarium. The floor is furnished with gravel, potted plants, moss, rocks, and perhaps an interestingly shaped branch or hollow log. Humidity can be maintained by regular spraying with a fine mist sprayer (remember to use only aged water or rainwater). An ideal heater for a terrarium is an aquarium heater placed in a tall jar of water, which can be concealed behind plants or logs. This setup also will help maintain humidity. The water in the jar will evaporate fairly quickly, so be sure you check and refill it frequently. There should be a perforated lid on the jar, and the heater cable should run through a small hole in it. This way, your amphibians won't get into the water and boil themselves.

Amphibians not given enough moisture in captivity often develop a sort of 'cocoon' around their bodies to protect themselves from drying up. Even then, they will perish if moisture is not provided at some point. Photo of an Ornate Horned Frog, *Ceratophrys ornata,* by Aaron Norman.

AMPHIBIAN NUTRITION

With only a few exceptions, amphibians are devotedly carnivorous. Most feed on a wide variety of invertebrates, including insects, spiders, crustaceans, mollusks, and worms. They will eat basically any invertebrate that will fit into their mouths. Only very large frogs and salamanders are capable of overpowering and eating small mammals and birds, and several species also will eat small fishes, reptiles, and even other amphibians if they're hungry enough. By taking such a variety of foodstuffs, wild amphibians ensure that they get the correct amount of proteins, carbohydrates, fats, vitamins and minerals. In other words, they get a balanced diet.

Many amphibians, especially frogs and toads, seem to have an unceasing appetite. This is because they are programmed to eat whatever they can when they can. Depending on

Virtually all amphibians are carnivorous and will take a variety of items, many of which can be obtained at your local pet shop. Photo of fly maggots by David J. Zoffer.

Although not often commercially available, grasshoppers make excellent food for amphibians. Photo by Mark Staniszewski.

Giant Mealworms, *Zoophobas atratus*, are commonly cultured for the pet trade and make acceptable supplementary meals for larger amphibians. Photo by David J. Zoffer.

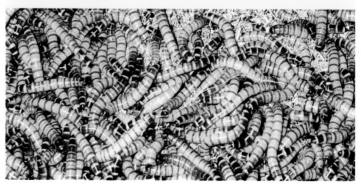

Crickets are the food item most often offered to captive amphibians. They can be obtained at many pet shops and provide amphibs with a great deal of nutrition. Photo by W. P. Mara.

Termites are often used as a staple food for amphibians that refuse crickets or are too small to take larger ones. You sometimes can find termites by turning over rotting logs. Photo by Isabelle Francais.

Aquatic worms and other aquatic 'bugs' usually solicit an enthusiastic feeding response from both fully aquatic amphibians and the larval and tadpole forms of land-dwelling species. Photo by Mark Staniszewski.

the state of their natural environment, food items may be bountiful or sparse. Amphibians, like most wild animals, try to really 'pack it away' during beneficial times so they then can get through the hard times without any problems.

Food Items

In order to keep our captive amphibians in the best of health, and to ensure that they do not fall victim to malnutrition, we must feed them a balanced diet, which can be defined as one that contains a variety of items. There are a few invertebrate foods that are produced commercially and thus may be obtained from pet shops and other outlets.

Crickets are one of the best-known and readily available livefoods. They are highly nutritious and usually are conveniently offered in a range of sizes. Hatchlings are about .12 in/3 mm long, whereas adult crickets are about 1 in/25 mm long.

Crickets can be kept in ventilated plastic containers (with holes small enough to prevent escape). They should be provided with crumpled paper or egg boxes to hide in and fed on a mixture of bran and oatmeal supplemented with a little greenfood or fruit. Water can be provided via a wet sponge in a shallow dish (which will need to be re-moistened regularly).

A little powdered vitamin/mineral supplement placed in the crickets' dry food will ensure that they remain healthy (this nutritional benefit also will be passed on to the amphibians). The food should be offered in shallow dishes (plastic jar lids are ideal) and replaced daily. Hygiene is just as important with livefood cultures as it is with the amphibians themselves. To breed crickets, provide them with dishes of a moist sand/peat mixture in which to lay their eggs. The eggs hatch after one week, and complete transformation from hatchling to adult takes about seven weeks.

Mealworms once were the staple diet of many pet insectivorous animals. Now they are known to be nutritionally incomplete because they are low in digestible calcium. However, they are readily available as a standby item and can be offered as a small part of

You can offer small rodents to larger amphibian specimens. Rodents are highly nutritious and can be procured, both live and frozen, at most pet shops. Photo by Isabelle Francais.

Aphids can be collected from the wild, but avoid areas that may have been treated with pesticides. Photo by Mark Staniszewski.

The Flour Beetle, *Tenebrio molitor*, is the adult form of the common mealworm. Only small beetle specimens should be used as amphibian food; larger ones often are well-armed and may be able to defend themselves. Photo by Michael Gilroy.

a more varied diet. Since mealworm breeding is a somewhat protracted affair, it is best to purchase them at your local pet shop. Those that you have bought can be stored in a ventilated plastic container in a deep layer of bran/oatmeal mixture with a piece of fresh potato or carrot offered daily for moisture.

Spiders can be collected and used as amphibian food, and they are very nutritious. But don't collect any until you are familiar with which species are and aren't dangerous. Some spiders can kill humans. Photo by Mark Staniszewski.

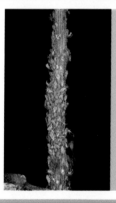

Flies can be collected in the wild using a trap baited with rotting meat. When holding large quantities of flies in captivity, be sure the enclosure is secure. Photo by Mark Staniszewski.

Waxworms are a relatively new discovery for herpetoculturists. They are the larvae of a moth which feeds on the wax in beehives and are a highly nutritious item for many amphibians (although they are a little fatty and thus, like mealworms, should be offered only as a supplement and not a staple). They can be purchased in small quantities as required.

Houseflies, bluebottles, greenbottles, and similar are an excellent food item for many frogs and toads. You can catch many of these in a fly trap baited with meat or fish. Alternatively, you may be able to purchase fly maggots (which can be used as a food item for larger species) and allow them to metamorphose into adult flies. Kept in a bran mixture, maggots will soon pupate and

You can collect earthworms by digging through moist soil or piles of wet leaves. Some keepers like to lay down swatches of wet burlap, which, after a day or so, will lure many worms to the surface. Photo by Mark Staniszewski.

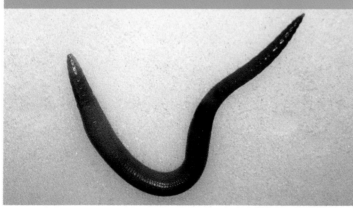

hatch as highly nutritious adults.

Grasshoppers, especially migratory locusts, may be obtainable through specialist suppliers. Adult locusts are relatively large and suitable only for larger amphibians. Various instar nymphs are smaller and useful for a range of smaller amphib specimens.

Fruitflies are a must for amphibian breeders. They are the very small flies that lay their eggs in decaying fruit. They are an excellent food item for newly metamorphosed frogs and salamanders, as well as the adults of the smaller species. You can obtain fruitflies that have been raised on agar jelly from biological suppliers. Alternatively, during the summer months, it is easy to collect your own fruitflies, especially if you live in the country. Put some banana skins or other decaying fruit in jars and place them in a sunny spot outside. The smell of the fruit will soon attract a number of flies, and you can capture them by quickly putting the lid on the jar. The insects are then transferred to the terrarium.

Commercial fish foods are commonly used with aquatic amphibians. Pellet foods work well with larger specimens, and flake foods are accepted by many in their larval stage. Photo of an African Clawed Frog, *Xenopus laevis*, by Isabelle Francais.

If you are an amphibian breeder, having a colony of fruitflies handy is an absolute necessity. Many neonatal amphibians won't be large enough (or willing enough) to take much else. Photo by Michael Gilroy.

Breeding your own livefoods certainly is possible, but it's considerably easier simply to obtain them from a pet shop. Those that aren't sold in pet shops can be collected in the wild. Photo of a Migratory Locust, *Locusta migratoria*, by Mark Staniszewski.

Most amphibians won't take food from your fingers, and in the case of some you shouldn't even try it! Large amphibs like this Tiger Salamander, *Ambystoma tigrinum*, for example, have powerful jaws and sharp teeth and can inflict painful bites. Photo by K. T. Nemuras.

Most adult amphibians can be fed two to three times per week; younger amphibs, three to four. Beware, however, that amphibians that have adapted to captive life will quickly become obese if given the chance. Photo of a Surinam Horned Frog, *Ceratophrys cornuta*, devouring a worm, by Mark Staniszewski.

Large quantities of mealworms can be maintained in captivity in a large plastic container filled with some type of bran or oatmeal material and a few pieces of fresh cut vegetable. Photo by Isabelle Francais.

One way of supplying your amphibians with a wonderful variety of livefood is to collect the food from your garden or the country. You will find an array of beetles, pillbugs, slugs, snails, and so on, under rocks, logs, or other ground litter. You also can collect this so-called 'meadow plankton' by passing a fine mesh net through grass and foliage. The catch should include small moths, beetles, bugs, grasshoppers, spiders and so on. These are size-graded and transferred to small jars for transport and storage.

Small insects can be collected from flower heads by using a 'pooter' or slurp gun, which is a glass or plastic bottle with a cork in the hole through which two glass or plastic tubes are passed. By placing the end of one tube in the flower head and sucking sharply on the other, the vacuum created will draw the insects into the bottle. A piece of gauze placed over the internal end of the sucking tube will stop you getting a mouthful of insects! Aphids can be collected simply by snapping off the shoot they are infesting and placing it in a jar.

Earthworms are an excellent food item and are accepted by many terrestrial and aquatic amphibians. You can collect them from moist soil simply by digging them up. Large numbers of earthworms often congregate in and around compost heaps. Such worms should be avoided, or at least suspected, because they may contain contaminants (from the compost pile) that could be toxic to your amphibians. If you think they might be infected, place them in a container of moist and sterile potting compost for a couple of days.

Tiny aquatic invertebrates are an important food item for many amphibian larvae, especially salamanders. For the tiniest amphibian larvae, brine shrimp can be used. You can buy brine shrimp eggs from aquarist suppliers and hatch them following the instructions on the package. Daphnia, or water fleas, are good for slightly larger larvae, and you also can buy them from aquarist suppliers. Some of the larger aquatic amphibians will take large aquatic

Most amphibians will accept caterpillars, which often can be collected right in your backyard or in a local patch of woodland. Photo by Mark Staniszewski.

Amphibian keepers need to give their animals food that is alive and moving around rather pre-killed, which is in direct opposition to the philosophy of most reptile-keepers, who prefer to train their animals to eat dead food. Photo of a locust by Michael Gilroy.

If you have a tank that contains a number of large amphibians, it may be prudent to remove some and feed them individually. This will reduce feelings of competition between the animals, not to mention possible instances of cannibalism. Photo of an African Bullfrog, *Pyxicephalus adspersus*, by Mark Staniszewski.

invertebrates such as water lice, freshwater shrimps, and small crayfish.

Some aquatic amphibians such as axolotls and clawed frogs will take non-live food items such as small pieces of lean meat or fish. These should be given in moderation and only supplied as a supplement to livefoods since most meats can be rather fatty and are unnatural for amphibs. However, the occasional 'meat treat' will do no harm (and also can be marinated in vitamin liquid to enhance its nutritional value).

Food Supplements

While a variety of food items should, theoretically at least, be adequate to provide a balanced diet, there may always be some gaps. Sometimes we are unable to provide a wide variety of items. Wildfood, for example, is not easy to find in the winter, and sometimes various cultivated foods may be in short supply.

But we can ensure that our amphibians do not suffer from malnutrition by providing them with a proprietary vitamin/mineral supplement. Special supplements for reptiles and/or amphibians are available through many pet shops. Powdered supplements are best, as they can be dusted over the feed insects before you give them to the amphibians. You will find that the fine particles of the powder will adhere readily to the insects' bodies. Vitamin supplements should not be given at every meal; every fifth is more sensible. Just as giving too few vitamins will cause problems, so will giving too many.

Feeding Strategies

Most amphibians should be fed at least every other day throughout the warmer months. Those that require a winter rest period should, of course, have their food intake reduced and ultimately stopped for the appropriate period in the winter. When feeding, only give enough food to satisfy the animal, not stuff it. Also, too many insects will infest the terrarium environment or drown in the water and spoil it.

Adding a little calcium powder to your amphibian's food will enhance the diet and possibly help fill gaps in their nutrition. Amphibians often suffer from an incomplete diet in captivity, so supplements are recommended. Photo courtesy of American Reptile.

CAPTIVE BREEDING

Only recently has the captive breeding of amphibians been seriously considered. At one time there seemed to be plenty of wild specimens to catch in order to keep the pet market supplied. Unfortunately, the demise of many species has made this practice an unreliable, and sometimes illegal, option. Thus, captive breeding has increased as a result of the combination of protective legislation for wild populations and the lure of commercial profits due to the continuing demand of the pet trade.

One reason why amphibians were rarely bred in the past is because hobbyists understood very little about their reproductive needs. A pair of frogs or salamanders were put in a cage (kept at the same temperature and humidity all year long) and probably fed on a inadequate diet. Such pets rarely survived for more than a few months, much less bred!

Most male anurans have a vocal sac on their throat that inflates each time the animal calls. If you're in the right place at the right time of year, you can hear dozens—sometimes hundreds—of males calling for mates. Photo of a Large-crested Toad, *Bufo cristatus*, by R. D. Bartlett.

Some male anurans have a pair of vocal sacs, one on either side of the throat, rather than a single sac that expands from the center. Photo of a pair of Carpenter Frogs, *Rana virgatipes*, by R. T. Zappalorti.

Breeding amphibians in captivity has only recently become popular. In many ways, it is more difficult than breeding reptiles, and less people do it because there isn't quite as large a market for amphibs as there is for reptiles. Photo of a calling Pine Woods Treefrog, *Hyla femoralis*, by R. D. Bartlett.

If you can afford it, buy male-female pairs rather than single specimens. That way, you can at least attempt to breed them. Captive-breeding may one day be the only way through which hobbyists will be able to obtain certain species. Photo of a pair of Marine, or Cane, Toads, *Bufo marinus*, by John Coborn.

If not for the efforts of captive-breeders worldwide, the herpetocultural community would never be able to marvel over many fascinating amphibian specimens, like this rare albino spadefoot toad, *Scaphiopus* sp. In the wild, such conspicuous animals don't live long. Photo by Isabelle Francais.

The most obvious advantage to the propagation of amphibians is that for every one produced in captivity, one less specimen needs to be taken from the wild. Photo of a calling Edible Frog, *Rana esculenta*, by Mark Staniszewski.

Today, however, we are in the situation where we can look upon the joint efforts of several generations of amphibian breeders, many of whom have been selfless enough to share their experiences by writing them down and then publishing them in various herpetological journals. Thus, we have been, and still are building up a store of amphibian-breeding knowledge, which will ultimately lead to the efficient propagation of all species.

The breeding of captive amphibians, in my opinion, is the most interesting and rewarding aspect of the herpetocultural hobby. Though some species can be considered fairly easy to breed, others constitute a true challenge. Apart from the pleasure achieved from captive breeding, there also is a moral obligation. Many frogs and salamanders now are bred in numbers sufficiently large enough to keep the pet trade satisfied, and in turn, there will be a reduction of specimens stolen from the wild.

Reproductive strategies among amphibian species vary depending on the climate. In general, amphibian species from temperate climates require a period of hibernation followed by the springtime increase of temperature and photoperiod. Amphibians from subtropical and tropical areas are more influenced by rain and humidity than temperature and photoperiod. Most of these types of amphibians breed during the rainy season. In some areas, where a regular rainy season cannot be relied upon, certain frogs may estivate in burrows for months, even years, before heavy rains permit a brief and hectic breeding frenzy.

Determination of the Sexes

In order to breed amphibians, you obviously need at least one male and one female of the species (there are a few species that breed asexually, but none worth mentioning here). With juvenile specimens, determination of sex often is difficult because there are no obvious external differences.

With adults, however, some observations can be made. In sexually mature newts and salamanders, the females

Many amphibians look their best during the breeding season. This is because they often have to 'dress up' in order to attract a mate. Shown here are three beautiful examples of breeding-season male newts of the genus *Triturus*. Top and middle, the Alpine Newt, *Triturus alpestris*. Bottom, the Marbled Newt, *Triturus marmoratus*. All photos by Mark Staniszewski.

Determining sex with some amphibians can be very difficult. Many display their differences only during the breeding season. Photo of a Banded Newt, *Triturus vittatus*, by Mark Staniszewski.

'Amplexus' is the term used to describe the mating position (also called the 'sexual embrace') of many male amphibians upon females. Photo of a pair of Golden Harlequin Frogs, *Atelopus zeteki*, by Mark Staniszewski.

There are two basic types of amplexus—*axillary*, where the male holds the female around the pectoral region, and *inguinal*, where the hold is around the pelvic region. Photo of a pair of Red-spotted Newts, *Notophthalmus viridescens viridescens*, by Mark Staniszewski.

are often larger and more robust than the males. The female's cloacal lips are relatively small, while those of the male will be notably swollen. In some of the aquatic newts (especially *Triturus* species), the males take on a colorful nuptial dress during the breeding season.

In adult frogs and toads, the females, again, often are larger and more robust than males, while the males of aquatic species often develop rough and dark-colored nuptial pads on the fingers during breeding season. The roughness of these pads helps the male grip the slippery female during amplexus. Male frogs call when they are ready to mate and have either a pair of balloon-like vocal sacs at the sides of the mouth, or a single sac on the throat. Even when not actually being used, the throat sac often can be revealed if you gently wrinkle the throat with your thumb and forefinger.

Knowing all this still does not help when you have half-grown specimens. In such cases it is best to acquire many specimens and raise them together in the hope that you have a selection of males and females.

Getting a Breeding Response

Temperate species should be given a winter rest period at reduced temperature and photoperiod, while feeding is suspended. This is not strictly hibernation but rather a substitute that seems to work quite well. Specimens kept warm and feeding all year are less likely to breed, and their lives are likely to be shorter.

The environment for the 'hibernation' period can consist of a period of two months at 50°F/ 10°C with a photoperiod reduced to around six hours of light each day. It is advisable to reduce the temperature and photoperiod gradually (over the course of, say, a week), then, when the rest period is over, increase in the same gradual fashion. Do not feed the animals during the rest period, and, after the rest period, remember to keep the cage humid and provide an adequate water body so breeding can take place in it.

Subtropical and tropical frogs are often brought into breeding condition by the onset of rains and increased humidity. To get them

The average caudate larva will only accept livefoods, like brine shrimp and bloodworms. These types of foods are available at many pet shops since they also are the food items preferred by many fish. Photo of a larval Blue Ridge Red Salamander, *Pseudotriton ruber nitidus*, by R. D. Bartlett.

Do not offer commercial fish foods to larval amphibs until they become active. Larvae that have just hatched may not eat, and in turn any foods you offer will serve only to pollute the water. Photo by Isabelle Francais.

The amount of time between hatching and metamorphosis varies from species to species, so you will need to know a little bit about the natural history of each species you have. It is crucial that you supply a land area for newly metamorphosed specimens to climb on. Photo of a larval Dusky Salamander, *Desmognathus fuscus*, by R. D. Bartlett.

into breeding condition you can still reduce the photoperiod and temperature, but not so much or as long as for temperate species.

The main requirement after the rest period is that the humidity is increased dramatically. You can use a special breeding tank containing about about 4 in/10 cm of aged water. Strained pond water can be used as is, but tapwater or rainwater must be allowed to stand for several days. Put in a few stones large enough so that they just break the surface, and perhaps one or two robust water plants. The best way to increase the air humidity is to create rain within the terrarium. This can be achieved by using using a circulatory pump or filter through a sprinkler. A perforated pipe suspended near the terrarium ceiling with the holes facing downward can be used to make the rain more lifelike.

About two weeks after the end of the rest period (and after the frogs have started feeding week again), place the 'breeders' in the rain chamber and start up the 'rain' for several hours each evening. This will cause many species to mate within a few days. As soon as you see signs of mating activity, you should then stop the 'rain.' The eggs will be laid shortly thereafter. Once that happens, you then can move the adults back to their regular quarters and use the 'rain chamber' as a rearing tank.

Rearing
Aquatic amphibian eggs need to be kept in well-aerated water. You should use an ordinary fish tank aerator with an airstone to assure this,

Most neonatal amphibians are remarkably tiny, whereas other species simply are so small, even the adults seem like babies. Photo of a Pink-headed Dwarf Caecilian, *Microcaecilia albiceps*, by Paul Freed.

Most anurans retain their tails for a short time after coming onto land (a day or so with most species). When they are still in their larval stage, the tail serves primarily as a rudder and a means of propulsion. Photo of a Bullfrog, *Rana catesbeiana*, by Mark Staniszewski.

and it also is advisable to have a filter so that the water is kept clean. As an extra safety measure, you can remove about a quarter of the water each day and replace it with clean (but aged) water. The water's temperature will vary depending on the species. As a general guide, use 65 to 72°F/18 to 22°C for temperate-region species and 75 to 86°F/24 to 30°C for tropical-region species. Most amphibian eggs will hatch in one to five days, but you should not add any foodstuffs to the tank until the larvae are swimming about freely.

Most frog and toad tadpoles can be reared on a high-quality tropical fish flake-food. Give the food very sparingly or else the water will become polluted.

Most salamander and newt larvae will take only livefoods, this consisting of tiny aquatic invertebrates. These often can be culled from pond water passed through a sieve. A good initial food for salamander larvae is brine shrimp, the eggs of which can be purchased from aquarist suppliers. These are hatched to the

supplier's directions. As the amphibian larvae increase in size, they can be given progressively larger food items. Other items you can offer include daphnia (water fleas), tubifex worms, and whiteworms.

Time from hatching to metamorphosis varies from species to species. Shortly before metamorphosis, you must be sure to provide accessible land areas so the newly transformed animals can easily leave the water. After this they can be placed in smaller versions of the adults' accommodations.

GENERAL AND MEDICAL CARE

At the present time, the study of diseases and treatment of captive amphibians is in its infancy. Although we know quite a bit about a few serious and not-so-serious diseases, prevention and treatment strategies are still far from satisfactory. Fortunately, the veterinary profession is now realizing the interest and value of researching and treating diseases of many of the lower vertebrates, and, hopefully, it will not be long before we can treat a sick frog or salamander just as efficiently as we can a sick cat or dog.

Most of the problems encountered in captive amphibians can be related to a captive environment that is less than optimum. Amphibians become stressed when they are kept in poor conditions, and stress is the precursor to greater disease susceptibility. Unclean cages, use of unsuitable cleaning chemicals, poor water quality, unsuitable temperature and photoperiod, poor diet, physical injuries, and frequent handling are all factors that contribute to stress. Efficient husbandry therefore is of the utmost importance if we are to prevent the onset of stress and stress-related problems.

Acquiring Healthy Stock

The single most important factor when acquiring new

The best way to deal with the health problems of captive amphibians simply is to avoid them in the first place—practice good husbandry. Once in their later stages, most amphibian health problems are nearly impossible to cure. Photo of an African Clawed Frog, *Xenopus laevis*, with dermal tuberculosis, by E. Elkan.

amphibians is to assure that they are as healthy as possible. If purchasing from a petshop or other dealer, you should consider the premises carefully and avoid establishments that display their animals in dirty, overcrowded conditions.

Also carefully inspect the animals you plan to purchase. Healthy amphibians should have moist skin that is free of any wounds, blemishes, inflammation, or discoloration. The eyes should be clear and bright, and the animal should be lively. In most cases, amphibians that don't struggle when handled are likely to be sick. If you are just starting out in the

Amphibians should be handled as infrequently as possible. Handling not only spreads germs from your hands to their skin, it also stresses the animals. Most amphibs don't care for handling very much. Photo of a Streamside Salamander, *Ambystoma barbouri*, by R. D. Bartlett.

amphibian-keeping hobby, take an experienced keeper with you when buying.

Handling

Amphibians generally aren't the type of pets that you would caress and cuddle; they are best only observed and admired. Having such a delicate and sensitive skin, most amphibians resent the warmth and saltiness of the human hand.

However, it will be necessary to handle your amphibians on certain occasions, such as when inspecting them for obvious signs of ill health or transferring them from one cage to another.

Aquatic amphibians and their larvae are best caught in a soft mesh net. You can examine them while in the net, lifting their bodies towards you by gently lifting them from underneath. However, they should be returned to the water as soon as possible.

When handling terrestrial amphibians, first rinse your hands in

Overcrowding is a common precursor to health problems in captive amphibians. It causes a great deal of stress and encourages enclosures to become filthy. Photo of Barking Treefrogs, *Hyla gratiosa*, by Isabelle Francais.

Be wary of any place that sells amphibians from overcrowded enclosures. There is a good chance the animal you buy will already be harboring some kind of health problem. Photo of albino African Clawed Frogs, *Xenopus laevis*, by Isabelle Francais.

During times when you must pick up one of your amphibians, be gentle and watch out not only for the animal but for yourself. Some amphibians, like this Ornate Horned Frog, *Ceratophrys ornata*, can deliver nasty bites. Photo by Isabelle Francais.

clean, warm (not hot) water and leave them wet. Small frogs and salamanders can be cupped in the hands and examined by spreading the fingers. It is best to hold them over a large bowl or tank of water so they have a safe place to land if they jump away from you. Large frogs and toads should be gripped around the waist, and their strong jumping legs should be restrained. Some of these animals are surprisingly strong and very slippery. Always hold the subject in its tank until you get a good grip and return it to its cage as soon as possible.

Transport

Once you have obtained an amphibian, it is important to get it to its destination as soon as possible. Aquatic amphibians can be carried in plastic bags pumped up with air and then sealed much in the same way pet fish are 'packaged.' Terrestrial amphibians can be placed in plastic bags or boxes containing loosely packed moist sphagnum moss or aquatic plants.

It is best to place all containers in an insulated container so the animals are protected from radical fluctuations in temperature during their journey.

Quarantine

Although you always want your new pets to be as healthy as possible when you acquire them, there is always the chance that one might be in the early stages of a disease whose symptoms have not yet appeared. If you have existing stock, it is important that this new stock is not mixed

Many amphibians secrete complex chemicals from their skin, many of which can be dangerous to humans if rubbed in the eyes or inadvertently ingested. *Always* wash your hands after handling amphibians. Photo by Isabelle Francais.

with it until a period of quarantine has elapsed. This consists of keeping the new animal(s) in a separate cage, and preferably in a different room, for a period of not less than three weeks. Provide the quarantine animals with all the necessary food and climatic requirements, and if, after the period of quarantine is over, the animals seem fit and healthy, you can introduce them to your existing stock.

Compatibility

Since many amphibians produce toxic secretions from their skin, it is best to house each species separately. The potency of these skin secretions varies from one species to another, so don't take chances by mixing your animals. Remember also that many amphibians have voracious appetites and will think nothing of devouring other specimens, even their own brothers and sisters! Therefore, only amphibians of similar size should be housed together.

General Hygiene

It is worth repeating here that humid environments within

Some amphibians are tamer than others. Most do not care for handling and will squirm about until set free. Others, like this beautiful Red-eyed Treefrog, *Agalychnis callidryas*, will sit calmly on your hand. Photo by Isabelle Francais.

Some amphibians are more compatible than others. Do yourself (and your pets) a favor and find out which ones need to be housed individually and which can be colonized. Photo of a Green Treefrog, *Hyla cinerea*, by Isabelle Francais.

Many amphibians can be transported via a plastic deli cup with some moistened paper toweling as a substrate and a few holes punched through the lid or sides. Photo of an albino Cranwell's Horned Frog, *Ceratophrys cranwelli*, by Isabelle Francais.

The simpler an enclosure arrangement is, the easier it will be to clean. Also, remember to use only mild soaps and disinfectants when cleaning. Residue from stronger materials may be absorbed through an amphibian's skin. Photo of horned frogs by Isabelle Francais.

furnishings should be thrown out and replaced or thoroughly scrubbed and rinsed. When cleaning the cage itself, do not use strong chemicals except in the case of a disease outbreak. Then, the cage and its furnishings should be disinfected using a 10% solution of warm water, dish soap, and a splash of household bleach. Afterwards, rinse everything *very thoroughly* in clean water.

Personal hygiene also should be taken into account. Always keep your hands scrupulously clean when handling amphibians, especially when you have several amphibian cages can provide ideal conditions for the proliferation of bacteria, fungi, and other unpleasant organisms. When setting up the enclosures, we must use materials that are as close to sterile as possible and try and attain a good balance between humidity and ventilation.

Enclosures should be cleaned at regular intervals. Decaying plants or plant parts should be removed, and the substrate and other

A filthy enclosure is a breeding ground for many health problems. It is advised that an enclosure be cleaned every time the keeper notices it's been dirtied. Photo by Isabelle Francais.

cages; there then is the danger of transferring a disease from one cage to the next. Remember also that some amphibians can carry pathogenic organisms (*Salmonella* for example), which you would not want to infect yourself with! Avoid touching your eyes during handling sessions so you don't spread amphibian toxins or bacteria to yourself.

Diseases and Treatment

Amphibians are most likely to suffer disease when their resistance is reduced by stress. These situations do occur, unfortunately, and you should learn how to deal with them when they do.

The following is a brief resume of the more commonly encountered maladies.

Wounds and Injuries: These commonly develop on frogs and toads while trying to escape and sometimes on salamanders that fight. Some larval amphibians have remarkable healing powers to the extent where whole limbs may be regenerated.

Open wounds are, of course, subject to bacterial or fungal infection, and antibiotic or antifungal treatment may become necessary.

Redleg is one of the most common amphibian afflictions. Once it has advanced to the stage seen in this African Clawed Frog, *Xenopus laevis*, chances are the animal will not survive. Caught in its earlier stages, however, it may be treatable (by a veterinarian). Photo by E. Elkan.

While cleaning an amphibian's enclosure, you can hold the occupant in a plastic bucket or a small fishbowl. Photo of an albino Cranwell's Horned Frog, *Ceratophrys cranwelli*, by Isabelle Francais.

A comparison between healthy and unhealthy—above, the Western Spadefoot Toad, *Scaphiopus hammondi*, is plump, brightly colored, wide-eyed, and alert. The specimen depicted below, however (a Couch's Spadefoot, *Scaphiopus couchi*), has lost so much body weight from a redleg infection that its pelvic girdle is clearly visible on the dorsum. The animal lived less than ten days after the photo was taken. Both photos by W. P. Mara.

Your veterinarian will be able to advise on the best course to take.

Nutritional Disorders: These may result from a deficiency of certain minerals or vitamins in the diet. Amphibians fed with a variety of foods and the occasional vitamin/mineral supplements are unlikely to develop any problems in this area.

Spring Disease: This often is a lethal disease and is caused by *Bacterium ranicida*, which is found mainly in temperate-region frogs during the breeding season. The symptoms include skin discoloration, lethargy, and gaping of the mouth. Antibiotic treatment may be successful if the disease is caught in its early stages.

Aeromonas Infection: Also called 'redleg,' an *Aeromonas hydrophila* infection manifests itself in reddening of the skin (especially on the thighs and lower body). Infected animals immediately should be isolated. Redleg often is lethal but may be treated if caught in its early stages. Immersion in a copper sulfate or potassium permanganate solution may help. Tetracycline has also been used with

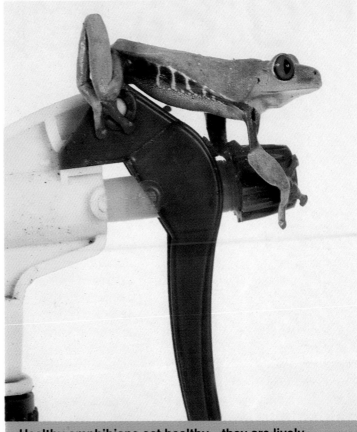

Healthy amphibians act healthy—they are lively, quick, and will try to get away from you if you taunt them. Photo of a Red-eyed Treefrog, *Agalychnis callidryas*, by Isabelle Francais.

some success. Your veterinarian should be able to advise you on the use of all necessary medications.

Fungus: Various fungal diseases can develop in amphibians, especially those that are largely or fully aquatic. One obvious symptom is areas of inflamed skin surrounded by whitish tissue.

Fungal infections should be treated by immersing the animal in a diluted solution of malachite green or mercurochrome (these products may be obtained under various trade names from aquarists' suppliers) for a few minutes, then repeating the procedure after 24 hours. A veterinarian should be consulted for exact details or visited if, after a day or so of treatment, no improvement occurs.

A SELECTION OF SALAMANDERS AND NEWTS

Mole Salamanders—Family Ambystomatidae

With only one genus (*Ambystoma*; *Rhyacosiredon* was recently synonymized) and about about 35 species, the Ambystomatidae form the mole salamanders of North America.

The **Axolotl, *Ambystoma mexicanum*,** is one of the best-known pet amphibians and has been bred extensively for many years. It is a good example of a neotenous amphibian, meaning the larvae do not metamorphose but instead remain aquatic and become sexually mature in their larval form. The wild form is known from lakes near Mexico City and is now protected (it should be noted that some experts believe there are none left in the wild). Maximum length is about 12 in/30 cm, though the average is somewhat smaller. The natural color is gray to brown, but olive, pied, and albino specimens are commonly available. The Axolotl has a robust body, a wide head, and a large mouth. There are two sets of three branched external gills on each side of the neck at the back of the head.

A pair of Axolotls will do well in a tank measuring 24 x 12 x 12 in/60 x 30 x 30 cm. The best substrate is a 2 in-/5 cm-deep layer of medium-grade aquarium gravel.

Since Axolotls are messy underwater feeders, it is best to have a power filter installed to keep the water clean. Axolotls will eat earthworms and the occasional maggot, mealworm, cricket, small fish, or strip of lean raw meat.

Axolotl, *Ambystoma mexicanum*. Albino specimen. Photo by Isabelle Francais.

Axolotl, *Ambystoma mexicanum*. Albino specimen. Photo by R. D. Bartlett.

Water temperature should be kept around 57 to 65°F/14 to 18°C (definitely no lower than 50°F/10°C) in the summer. A winter cooling period for a couple of months at around 48°F/9°C, will probably induce a breeding response in the spring.

The **Tiger Salamander, *Ambystoma tigrinum,*** is the world's largest terrestrial salamander, with an average length of between 6 and 13.5 in/15.2 and 34.2 cm. It has a wide range in North America and is a popular and hardy pet. There are several subspecies, some of which are endangered and therefore protected. Colors vary, but most specimens are either brown or olive and marked with irregular stripes, blotches, or spots in brown, yellow, gray, or cream.

Tiger Salamanders require a large

Barred Tiger Salamander, *Ambystoma tigrinum mavortium*. Larval form. Photo by Aaron Norman.

Sonoran Tiger Salamander, *Ambystoma tigrinum stebbinsi.* Photo by R. D. Bartlett.

aquaterrarium (mostly land) with adequate hiding places. Maintain the temperature at 59 to 77°C/15 to 25°C, reducing it for a few weeks in winter. Feed the Tigers on a variety of invertebrates. Large specimens will be able to take "pinky" mice. Larval specimens can be kept in a manner similar to Axolotls.

The **Spotted Salamander,** *Ambystoma maculatum,* is another popular North American species. It bears some resemblance to the commonly kept Fire Salamander, *Salamandra salamandra,* by having yellow or orange spots and/or blotches on a dark (usually black or very dark brown) ground color. Most keepers consider it a

hardy and long-lived species if properly cared for. It occurs throughout eastern North America from Canada south to just north of the Gulf Coast. Captive specimens require a large woodland terrarium with plenty of hiding places, high

humidity, and a small water body (which should be broadened if you wish to breed them). They will feed on a variety of invertebrates.

Other North American mole salamanders that occasionally are kept include the the Small-mouthed Salamander, *A. texanum;* the Marbled Salamander, *A. opacum;* the Northwestern Salamander, *A. gracile;* and the Long-toed Salamander, *A. macrodactylum.* All require captive conditions similar to those described for the Tiger Salamander.

American Giant Salamanders—Family Dicamptodontidae

These once were classified in the family Ambystomatidae, and

Spotted Salamander, *Ambystoma maculatum.* Photo by K. T. Nemuras.

Spotted Salamander, *Ambystoma maculatum*. Photo by Mark Staniszewski.

some taxonomists believe they should have stayed there. However, members of the one genus, *Dicamptodon* (with about four species), have several characteristics that distinguish them from the mole salamanders.

The **Pacific Giant Salamander,** ***Dicamptodon ensatus,*** probably is the best-known member of the group. It is a large species, reaching about 11 in/27 cm. It occurs in extreme western North America from southern Canada to central coastal California. It also is found in the Rocky Mountains in Idaho and extreme west-central Montana (these populations now represent a separate species, *D. aterrimus*).

It is husky, smooth-skinned, and brown to

California Giant Salamander, *Dicamptodon ensatus*. Photo by Mark Staniszewski.

Cope's Giant Salamander, *Dicamptodon copei.* Larval form. Photo by R. D. Bartlett.

occurs in the extreme northwestern United States. Growing to a length of 4.5 in/11.4 cm, it has bulging eyes set high on its head and a laterally flattened tail. The slender body is colored plain brown or mottled olive above, while the belly is yellowish green or yellowish orange with dark flecks.

This is a 'difficult' captive and therefore best suited only for the advanced hobbyist. It needs a cool, rocky aquaterrarium with fast-moving water and a muddy substrate. It also requires small insects and spiders.

purplish with dark mottling on the dorsum and light brown to cream on the belly. It is a fairly unusual salamander in that it can emit a low-pitched yelp when disturbed.

It requires a cool woodland aquaterrarium with flowing water and plenty of hiding spots, plus a few branches or sturdy plants (believe it or not, this animal occasionally climbs). It will take a wide variety of foods, including various insects, spiders, small mice, and even small snakes. Do not keep small specimens together with large ones; the latter may eat the former.

Olympic Salamanders—Family Rhyacotritonidae

Also a former member of the Ambystomatidae, the genus *Rhyacotriton* has since been given its own family and contains three species.

The best-known member of the group probably is the **Olympic Salamander, *Rhyacotriton olympicus,*** which

Lungless Salamanders—Family Plethodontidae

With about 29 genera and well over 250 species, this is the largest

Olympic Salamander, *Rhyacotriton olympicus*. Photo by R. D. Bartlett.

and most complex salamander family. Found primarily in North, Central, and South America, new species and subspecies are still being described fairly regularly. Most are slender-bodied and lack lungs, respiring instead through the skin.

The **Red Salamander, Pseudotriton ruber,** is one of the most beautiful plethodontids. Reaching a maximum length of about 7 in/17.7 cm, the most colorful form is bright orange-red with a peppering of small black spots. Older specimens tend to be orange-brown to purplish brown. The belly is pinkish and may or may not have dark spots.

Blackchin Red Salamander, *Pseudotriton ruber schencki*. Photo by R. D. Bartlett.

This is one of the trickier plethodontids to maintain, due mainly to its delicacy and the fact that it requires cool, moving water. The terrarium should be unheated, have high humidity, and offer many hiding places. Most captive specimens seem to enjoy earthworms, but a variety of other invertebrates also should be offered until a sufficiently broad diet is realized.

The **Mountain Dusky Salamander, Desmognathus ochrophaeus,** is a fairly widespread species, found west of the Hudson River in New York to northeastern Georgia and in northeastern Alabama. It reaches a maximum adult length of 4.5 in/ 11.4 cm. The color varies through a range of browns, yellows, oranges, grays, and greens. The patterns vary through thick or narrow-edged blotches or spots, chevrons, stripes, and zigzags down the back.

Southern Red Salamander, *Pseudotriton ruber vioscai*. Photo by R. D. Bartlett.

Blue Ridge Red Salamander, *Pseudotriton ruber nitidus*, by R. D. Bartlett.

Blue Ridge Red Salamander, *Pseudotriton ruber nitidus*, by R. D. Bartlett.

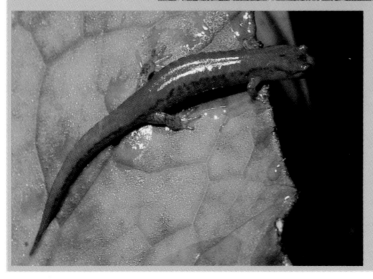

Mountain Dusky Salamander, *Desmognathus ochrophaeus*. Photo by R. D. Bartlett.

Mountain Dusky Salamander, *Desmognathus ochrophaeus*. Photo by W. P. Mara.

Seal Salamander, *Desmognathus monticola*. Photo by R. D. Bartlett.

Monterey Ensatina, *Ensatina eschscholtzi eschscholtzi*. Photo by Aaron Norman.

This and other species in the genus require a cool aquaterrarium, preferably with artificial seepage. In nature, eggs are laid on land but near water, and the mother tends to her nest. Upon hatching, the larvae enter the water.

The **Ensatina, *Ensatina eschscholtzi,*** has several subspecies and is found in extreme southwestern Canada, south along the western coast of the USA, and then into Baja. Reaching a length of about 6 in/ 15.2 cm, it exhibits a broad range of colors and patterns, including browns and reddish browns with cream, yellow, or orange spots. One of its most outstanding physical qualities is its large round eyes.

Ensatinas like a cool, moist terrarium, preferably furnished with living plants and mosses and plenty of hiding places. They feed on a variety of small invertebrates. Eggs are laid underground, and the female will brood the hatch. Complete metamorphosis occurs before hatching, and sexual maturity will be reached in around three years.

Jordan's Salamander, *Plethodon jordani,* is one of the more attractive members of its genus. It is found in the southern Appalachians, from southwestern Virginia to eastern Tennessee and western North Carolina to northeastern Georgia and northwestern South Carolina. It varies greatly in color and pattern throughout its range, so much so that early herpetologists thought there were multiple species and subspecies.

Sierra Nevada Ensatina, *Ensatina eschscholtzi platensis*. Photo by Mark Staniszewski.

The basic color is black above with gray below, with small white spots on the sides and cheeks. The chin usually is light-colored. Specimens from the Great Smokies have red cheek patches, while those from the Nantahala Mountains have red limbs.

Jordan's Salamander, *Plethodon jordani*. Photo by R. D. Bartlett.

These salamanders, and other members of the genus, require cool, moist accommodations, furnished with plants, mosses, and adequate hiding places. They will feed on a variety of small invertebrates. There is no aquatic stage, and the eggs are laid in underground cavities.

Newts and Fire Salamanders—Family Salamandridae

The family contains about 14 genera and about 53 species. Most genera are found in Eurasia and North Africa; only two occur in North America.

The **Fire Salamander, *Salamandra salamandra***, is the 'original' salamander of Europe and was the inspiration for much early folklore in the countries in which it occurs. With a maximum length of about 10 in/25 cm, it occurs over much of the central and southwestern Palearctic Region. It has a beautiful pattern of bright yellow to orange stripes, blotches, or spots on a black background. There are quite a few subspecies currently recognized.

The Fire Salamander makes a good terrarium

Jordan's Salamander, *Plethodon jordani "clemsonae."* Photo by R. D. Bartlett.

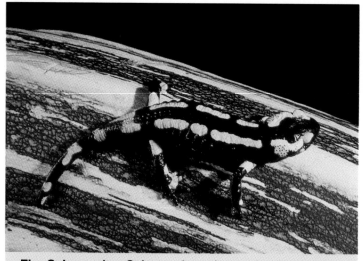

Fire Salamander, *Salamandra salamandra*. Photo by M. P. and C. Piednoir.

color is brownish-black, with the vertebral stripe, head, limbs, tail, and parotid glands all being orange or rusty brownish red, either bright or dull.

Care for this animal is similar to that previously described for the Fire Salamander; a daytime temperature of around 77°F/25°C reduced to

subject; in optimum conditions it will live for many years (up to 50 has been recorded). It requires a cool, moist, and well-planted terrarium with adequate hiding places and a shallow pool of water. Daily mistings will keep humidity high, and temperature should not be allowed to rise over 68°F/20°C. Most specimens are voracious

and will accept a wide variety of standard terrestrial-salamander foods. Mating occurs on land, usually in spring or early summer. The female deposits well-grown, bronze-colored larvae in a suitable pool or stream.

The **Crocodile Newt, *Tylototriton verrucosus,*** is native to parts of India, Indo-China, and western China. It grows to a maximum length of about 6.4 in/16 cm and has some unusual features to its stocky body. There is a heavy vertebral stripe that is slightly keeled, an arrow-shaped head (with large parotid glands on either side), and a row of obvious nodules along each flank. The basic

Crocodile Newt, *Tylototriton verrucosus.* Photo by Aaron Norman.

68°F/20°C at night is one of the few differences. A winter rest period at slightly cooler temperatures should induce breeding in the spring.

The **Crested Newt, *Triturus cristatus*,** is one of Europe's largest newts, some specimens growing to a length of around 8 in/20 cm. It inhabits much of Europe but is replaced in southeastern France and Spain by the attractive Marbled Newt, *T. marmoratus.*

T. cristatus is at its

Fire Salamander, *Salamandra salamandra*. Photo by M. P. and C. Piednoir.

visual best in the mating season (in the spring), when the male takes on his courtship dress. For most of the year these newts live in sheltered, moist situations on land. In the spring and early summer, however, they congregate in and around their breeding pools. The normally drab brownish color of both the male and the female becomes jet black with a scattering of white spots along the flanks, contrasting strongly with the (permanent) black-spotted, orange-red belly. The males also develop a jagged dorsal crest and a bluish white stripe on either side of the tail.

After an elaborate courtship and mating ceremony, the female lays her eggs singly, each attached to the underside of a leaf of an aquatic plant.

T. cristatus should be kept in a large, unheated aquaterrarium with plenty of plants in the water. They can be fed a variety of small, live invertebrates. During their aquatic stage, they will feed on aquatic insects, earthworms, and so on.

Several other European newts in the genus, including the aforementioned Marbled

Crocodile Newt, *Tylototriton verrucosus*. Photo by K. T. Nemuras.

Newt, *T. marmoratus*; the Common Newt, *T. vulgaris*; the Palmate Newt, *T. helveticus*; the Alpine Newt, *T. alpestris*; and the diminutive Italian Newt, *T. italicus*, have similar breeding habits and can be kept as described for *T. cristatus*.

The **Eastern Newt, *Notophthalmus viridescens***, occurs all throughout the eastern half of the USA. It grows to a length of around 5.5 in/14 cm and has a wide range of colors and markings.

The best known probably is the Red-spotted Newt, *N. v. viridescens*, which is normally olive-brown marked with a series of

Crested Newt, *Triturus cristatus*. Larval form. Photo by R. D. Bartlett.

Marbled Newt, *Triturus marmoratus*. Photo by R. D. Bartlett.

Red-spotted Newt, *Notophthalmus viridescens viridescens*. Photo by Mark Staniszewski.

small, black-bordered red spots. The land-dwelling form, called the 'Red Eft,' is orange-red in color.

Eastern Newts can be kept in a moist and unheated aquaterrarium furnished with plants, mosses, flat stones, and a variety of hiding places. They will eat a variety of small invertebrates (Red Efts can be stubbornly fastidious in the area of feeding). The closely related Striped Newt, *N. perstriatus*, and the Black-spotted Newt, *N. meridionalis*, have similar

Red-spotted Newt, *Notophthalmus viridescens viridescens*. 'Red Eft.' Photo by Mark Staniszewski.

habits and require similar care.

The **California Newt, *Taricha torosa,*** occurs only in California. Growing to a length of around 7 in/18 cm, its rough skin is tan to reddish brown above and yellow to orange on the belly. *Torosa* is terrestrial outside the breeding season, and breeds in water in the spring. Care and feeding is similar to that previously described for *N. viridescens.*

California Newt, *Taricha torosa*. Photo by Aaron Norman.

Mudpuppies and Waterdogs—Family Proteidae

This family contains two genera and about six species, five of which occur in the USA. A single genus, *Proteus*, occurs in Europe.

The **Mudpuppy, *Necturus maculosus,*** is perhaps the best-known member of the family. It is a relatively large salamander, maxing out

California Newt, *Taricha torosa*. Photo by R. D. Bartlett.

at around 17 in/43.1 cm. It is totally aquatic and possesses feathery, maroon-colored stalks on either side of the head. It is gray to rusty brown above, with dark-bordered bluish blotches.

Mudpuppies can be kept in a large, unheated aquarium with filtered and aerated water, rocks, and tree roots (in view of the Mudpuppy's powerful digging talents, planting is usually a waste of time). They can be fed small fishes, water snails, freshwater shrimp, and other aquatic animals.

Mudpuppy, *Necturus maculosus*. Photo by K. T. Nemuras.

A SELECTION OF FROGS AND TOADS

Considering the vast number of anuran species in the world, it simply is impractical to try to usefully discuss any more than a few choice examples in a volume of this size. I therefore have endeavored to examine only those species that are likely to be kept in the vivarium plus a few others which may be of special interest.

Wood Frog, *Rana sylvatica*. Photo by David Green.

Typical Frogs—Family Ranidae

This family contains over 600 species in more than 50 genera and includes the well-known temperate-region frogs of the genus *Rana* as well as many lesser-known species from various parts of the tropics. Ranidae is distributed worldwide with only a few exceptions.

The **Wood Frog, *Rana sylvatica*,** is a well-known North American species that occurs over a great deal of the USA (mostly in the northeastern quarter) and well into Canada.

Growing to a maximum length of around 3.25 in/ 8.3 cm, it is pinkish, tan, or light brown, with a light stripe along the upper jaw and a prominent dark mask which ends at the eardrum.

This is a very cold-tolerant species that will breed in early spring, often before the ice has completely melted. It is thus suitable for outdoor enclosures in cooler areas, or moist and unheated vivaria kept in a cool situation. It should be allowed to hibernate during the coldest part of

winter. It is fairly easy to breed if you have a colony of specimens.

The **Leopard Frogs, *Rana pipiens*** complex, form a group of interesting and colorful

Leopard Frog, *Rana pipiens*. Photo by Aaron Norman.

frogs variously colored and marked. They grow to around 5 in/12.7 cm. Various forms can be found as far north as Canada and throughout the USA. Northern forms can be kept in unheated accommodations, but southern forms will require varying amounts of warmth depending on their origin. Most *pipiens* frogs are voracious and hardy, taking a variety of food items and living long lives.

Bullfrog, *Rana catesbeiana*. Photo by Aaron Norman.

The **Bullfrog, *Rana catesbeiana,*** is primarily found throughout the eastern USA and has been widely introduced to the western half as well. It is the largest North American frog, growing to around 8 in/20 cm. It is green to yellowish above, mottled with dark gray, while the underside is whitish.

The Bullfrog is perhaps best-suited for an enclosed garden pool since it likes deep water. If kept indoors, it will require a large aquaterrarium with the water at least 18 in/45.7 cm deep. Maintain the temperature at around 68 to 72°F/20 to 22°C during the summer and provide a cooling period during the winter. It will feed on a variety of large invertebrates, including crickets, grasshoppers, earthworms, snails. Small fish and small mice may also be taken.

The **Pig Frog, *Rana grylio,*** gets its common name from its piglike grunt. Growing to over 6 in/15.2 cm, it is more aquatic than its close relative the Bullfrog. It has a very large eardrum and fully webbed hind feet. Its color varies from olive green to gray-green or dark brownish, with darker spots on the body and banding on the thighs.

Pig Frogs once were hunted for food (their legs supposedly are very tasty), and perhaps they have learned from this, for they are extremely wary! Native primarily to the Gulf Coast states of the U. S., they require a warm vivarium with deep water and a small land area. Water temperature should be maintained at around 77°F/25°C in the summer, cooled to 66°F/ 19°C in the winter. Pig Frogs can be fed on a

Bullfrog, *Rana catesbeiana*. Albino specimen. Photo by K. T. Nemuras.

variety of invertebrates, including crayfish.

There are many more 'keepable' North American frogs in the genus *Rana*, including the Green Frog, *Rana clamitans*; the Pickerel Frog, *Rana palustris* (which cannot be kept with other species due to its toxicity); and the Carpenter Frog, *Rana virgatipes*.

A number of European *Rana* species also are occasionally kept in the vivarium—

The **European Grass Frog** is one example. It was described as ***Rana temporaria*** by Linnaeus back in 1758. It occurs throughout northern, central, and eastern Europe and into the Arctic Circle in the north.

Growing to a maximum of 4 in/10 cm, its color

may be reddish, whitish, gray, brown, or yellow, marked and striped with brown, or black. There is a large and dark ear patch.

Though it does reasonably well in an unheated vivarium (captive specimens have lived over 12 years) it is perhaps better-suited to an outdoor enclosure with a pond, especially if you want it to breed. It is mainly terrestrial, living in moist, vegetated areas. It feeds on a variety of invertebrates and is especially fond of worms, slugs, and snails.

The European green-

European Grass Frog, *Rana temporaria*. Photo by David Green.

frog complex includes the **Edible Frog, *Rana esculenta,*** which is found throughout western and central Europe. It has also been introduced successfully into a few areas of England.

Reaching a length of 4

in/10 cm, it is variable in color, but it usually is bright green with brownish stripes and patches. It is much more aquatic than the aforementioned European Grass Frog and therefore requires an aquaterrarium with deep water or, again, an outdoor pool. It feeds on a variety of invertebrates captured both above and below water.

The **Marsh Frog, *Rana***

Edible Frog, *Rana esculenta*. Photo by L. Wischnath.

ridibunda, is a larger species, growing to 5 in/ 12.7 cm, and occurs in central and eastern Europe. It is usually greenish above with large dark patches. Its habits and care are similar to those of the American Bullfrog.

Turning to a couple of other genera in the family Ranidae, it is worth mentioning the world's largest frog, the

Marsh Frog, *Rana ridibunda*. Photo by George Dibley.

Goliath Frog, *Conraua goliath*. Very aquatic, it occurs in the higher-elevation jungle streams of central West Africa. Growing to a length of 12 in/30 cm, it is an intriguing animal but rarely turns up in the hobby. If you do manage to obtain one, remember that it requires a deep water body with a few sturdy land areas. Water temperature should be maintained at about 77°F/25°C, and the diet should consist of small fishes and aquatic crustaceans.

The **African Bullfrog,**

Goliath Frog, *Conraua goliath*. Photo by Paul Freed.

Pyxicephalus adspersus, grows to a length of around 8 in/20 cm. It is mainly greenish above, with a series of ridges running down its back. It is creamy white on the belly, with bright yellow or orange patches where the limbs join the body.

It requires a terrarium with a deep substrate (gravel and leaf litter work well), into which it will burrow with just the top of the head showing as it waits to "ambush" any vertebrate food you may give it. It has many characteristics similar to the unrelated South

African Bullfrog, *Pyxicephalus adspersus.* Photo by Mark Staniszewski.

African Bullfrog, *Pyxicephalus adspersus.* Photo by W. P. Mara.

American horned frogs (genus *Ceratophrys*), including its capacity to eat until it literally can't move. And since this frog is cannibalistic, it is best to keep specimens singly.

Treefrogs—Family Hylidae

Most hylids have broad, sucker-like toe pads that enable them to better manage their arboreal lifestyle. A few, however, are highly terrestrial. The family contains around 37

Green Treefrogs, *Hyla cinerea.* Photo by Isabelle Francais.

genera and over 600 species.

The **Green Treefrog, *Hyla cinerea,*** is one of the best-known members of its genus and often is the species the beginning hobbyist starts with. Occurring in the southeastern USA, it grows to about 2 in/5 cm. It is predominantly green in color, often with a narrow white stripe extending from the lower lip usually to the hind limb.

It requires a tall, moist, and well-planted terrarium with a temperature of around 77 to 80°F/25 to 27°C during the day and a slight reduction at night. A winter cooling period followed by the provision of a deep water area and an increase in humidity is required for breeding (even then, it should be

Gray Treefrog, *Hyla versicolor*. Photo by W. P. Mara.

noted, this species is very difficult to propagate). It will feed on a variety of small invertebrates.

The **Gray Treefrog, *Hyla versicolor*,** is another fairly common species. It occurs primarily in the eastern USA but also reaches into southern Canada. It is similar in size to the preceding species and is usually a mottled gray or greenish gray with bright orange or yellowish flash colors on the inner thighs. It requires similar care to that described for *H. cinerea*.

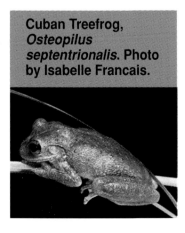

Cuban Treefrog, *Osteopilus septentrionalis*. Photo by Isabelle Francais.

The **Cuban Treefrog, *Osteopilus septentrionalis*,** can exceed 3.5 in/8.8 cm in length. A native of Cuba, it has been successfully introduced into Florida and Puerto Rico. It has a broad head and large eyes. The skin is rough and there are relatively large digital disks. The colors range through browns, yellows, and greens. The males develop a distinct greenish tinge during the breeding season.

Specimens require a tall, moist, and well-planted terrarium with sturdy climbing branches and plants. Maintain the temperature at 77 to 84°F/25 to 29°C, reducing it to around 68°F/20°C at night. Offer a variety of invertebrates.

White's Treefrog, *Litoria caerulea*, occurs in Australia and New Guinea. It has earned enormous popularity as a pet in many parts of the world due to its cute plumpness and friendly disposition. A large specimen can reach 5 in/ 12.5 cm in length. The color is bluish to leaf green, sometimes with a number of small white spots on the back. Specimens are frequently bred in captivity and are usually available. They

White's Treefrogs, *Litoria caerulea*. Photo by Isabelle Francais.

have similar requirements to the Cuban Treefrog previously mentioned.

True Toads—Family Bufonidae

The family Bufonidae contains around 25 genera and over 350 species.

White's Treefrogs, *Litoria caerulea*. Photo by Isabelle Francais.

Woodhouse's Toad, *Bufo woodhousi*, is one of the best-known North American toad species. It reaches a maximum length of around 4 in/10 cm. It ranges throughout the USA and is able to survive in a variety of habitats. The subspecies *B. w. fowleri* is very popular due to its attractive coloration—brown or gray (sometimes greenish or brick red, although rarely) with a light stripe down the middle of the back. There sometimes are small reddish spots on the dorsum, especially on the flanks and limbs.

This species requires a cool (room temperature) and semi-humid terrarium with a few potted plants and some hiding places. A small

Woodhouse's Toad, *Bufo woodhousi woodhousi*. Photo by Ken Lucas.

water dish will be adequate outside the breeding season. The diet can be made up of a wide variety of invertebrates.

Other North American species requiring similar care include the American Toad, *B. americanus*; the Great Plains Toad, *B. cognatus*; the Canadian Toad, *B. hemiophrys*; and the Green Toad, *B. debilis*.

The **European Green Toad**, *Bufo viridis*, is a relatively popular pet

European Grass Toad, *Bufo viridis*. Photo by Mark Staniszewski.

amphibian in parts of continental Europe and occasionally turns up in the USA. Growing to about 4 in/10 cm, its background color is cream to brown and marked with vivid green patches.

It requires a semi-humid terrarium outside the breeding season and a small water dish. Raise temperature to 81°F/27°C during the summer (reduce at night) and allow a short period of cool hibernation in the winter. Feed on a variety of invertebrates.

The **Marine,** or **Cane Toad,** *Bufo marinus*, is

Marine, or Cane, Toad, *Bufo marinus*. Photo by W. P. Mara.

a true giant among toads, with large females recorded in excess of 9 in/22.8 cm, though most are somewhat smaller. Typically toadlike in profile, this species makes an excellent pet and is usually available, though it is a prohibited animal in some places for fear that it will escape and colonize the surrounding countryside.

Marine Toads occur naturally in northern South America and Central America, just barely reaching into the USA. They have become feral in other parts of the world.

Marine, or Cane, Toad, *Bufo marinus*. Photo by R. D. Bartlett.

The Marine Toad requires a large terrarium with a substantial body of water in which it will soak regularly. Maintain temperature around 82°F/28°C during the day, reducing to about 68°F/20°C at night. Feed on a variety of large invertebrates and small mice.

Clawed Frogs—Family Pipidae

This is a small but interesting family with five genera and around 27 species. They are all almost exclusively aquatic and are ideal subjects for anyone interested in the aquarium hobby, particular anyone who has always had an interest in fish and now wants to dabble in the herp-keeping field.

The **Surinam Toad**, *Pipa pipa*, from slow-moving rivers of northern South America, has a most bizarre appearance. It has a flattened body, and a pointed snout at the front of a triangular head. The fingers are tipped with sensory, star-like appendages that help it find food by touch since its habitat is so murky. The hind limbs are powerful, and all four feet strongly webbed, making this animal an agile swimmer. It is a mottled gray-brown in color above, pale white or extremely light brown beneath.

A pair should be housed in a large aquarium (not less than 25 gallons/150 liters) with a water depth of 12 in/30 cm. Use a water filter and change a jugful

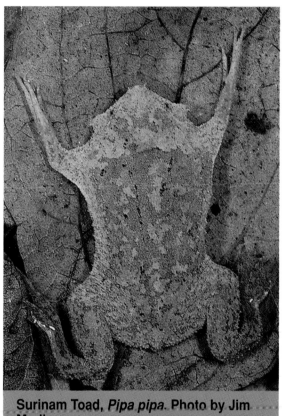

Surinam Toad, *Pipa pipa*. Photo by Jim Merli.

of water every other day. Maintain the water temperature around 83°F/26°C. Feed them on small live fish (such as guppies), strips of lean meat (not too much of this), and earthworms. The breeding habits are interesting in that the young metamorphose in little chambers in the thick, spongy skin of the female's back.

The **African Clawed Frog**, *Xenopus laevis*, occurs naturally in muddy, slow-moving watercourses in eastern and southern Africa and has been successfully introduced into other parts of the world, including southern California. With a maximum length of 5 in/12.5 cm, it has long been propagated for both the hobby and the medical trade (for experimental purposes) and is an excellent subject for the beginner since it is quite hardy and easy to keep. A pair can be kept in a fashion similar to the previously discussed *Pipa pipa*.

Poison Frogs—Family Dendrobatidae

This family contains the living jewels of the amphibian world. There are about 120 species, occurring in Central and South America. All are relatively small. Many

African Clawed Frogs, *Xenopus laevis*. Albino and normal-colored specimens. Photo by Isabelle Francais.

Dyeing Poison Frog, *Dendrobates tinctorius*. Photo by U. E. Friese.

Blue Poison Frog, *Dendrobates azureus*. Photo by R. D. Bartlett.

species are breathtaking in color and pattern and, as such, are popular terrarium subjects.

The bright colors are designed to warn predators that they are poisonous. The skin secretions of some species are so poisonous, in fact, that they have been used by many natives to coat the tips of their poison darts.

Dendrobatids reproduce on land, the eggs often being laid on a leaf or stone on the forest floor. The male sometimes guards the eggs after fertilizing them and, when they hatch, he transports the tadpoles on his back to water, usually to a small pool or the water reservoir in a bromeliad cup.

To describe two popular examples, the "pallid" form of the

Dyeing Poison Frog, *Dendrobates tinctorius*, from Surinam, has a blue and yellow body marked with shiny black patches, while the limbs are a deep magenta blue or yellow with black spots. The **Green Poison Frog, *D. auratus*,** is patterned

Green Poison Frog, *Dendrobates auratus*. Photo by R. D. Bartlett.

with enamel-black blotches on an almost metallic green background.

Most dendrobatids can be housed in a tall and humid rainforest-type terrarium furnished with tree branches, tropical plants, and a small waterpool. If you supply bromeliads, the frogs are more likely to breed, though some will do just as well with small water containers. Maintain temperature at about 80°F/26°C during the day, reducing to 72°F/22°C at night, and spray regularly with rainwater or aged tapwater. Offer small insects such as fruitflies and newly hatched crickets as food.

For more detailed information on these fascinating animals,

look for these two excellent TFH books by experienced author Jerry G. Walls—*Keeping Poison Frogs* (RE-108), and *Jewels of the Rainforest—Poison Frogs of the Family Dendrobatidae* (TS-223).

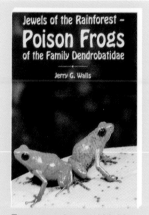

For a complete and highly colorful study of the poison frogs, get a copy of Jerry G. Walls's *Jewels of the Rainforest—Poison Frogs of the Family Dendrobatidae* (TS-223).

Marbled Reed Frog, *Hyperolius marmoratus*. Photo by Ken Lucas.

Reed and Grass Frogs—Family Hyperoliidae

This family consists of around 18 genera and about 220 species. It is native to Africa and some of the Indian Ocean islands. Some members of the genus *Hyperolius* are attractively colored and are occasionally available.

The **Marbled Reed Frog, *Hyperolius marmoratus*,** is perhaps the best-known species. Growing to just 1.5 in/4 cm, it occurs over much of sub-Saharan Africa. There is a complex of subspecies, so colors and patterns vary enormously. There are greens, browns, yellows, and blues, and they may be marbled, blotched, striped, spotted, or a mixture of any combination.

Reed frogs require a tall terrarium with plenty of reed-like plants. Maintain a temperature of 72 to 82°F/22 to 28°C and a high humidity (regular mist spraying, or drip system), and offer a variety of small invertebrates.

Tropical Frogs—Family Leptodactylidae

There are about 50 genera and over 750 species in this large South American family. Some of the best-known members are the horned

West African reed frog, *Hyperolius* sp. Photo by Paul Freed.

frogs of the genus *Ceratophrys.*

The **Ornate Horned Frog,** *Ceratophrys ornata,* is one of the of greens and browns. Notable is the fleshy horn over each eye, giving the animal its name. 72°F/22°C at night. Specimens are best housed singly unless you are breeding them. They can be offered large

Ornate Horned Frog, *Ceratophrys ornata.* Photo by Mark Staniszewski.

Ornate Horned Frog, *Ceratophrys ornata*. Photo by M. P. and C. Piednoir.

ogres of frogdom. It has a large head complimented by an enormous gape, and it will eat anything that fits into its mouth. It reaches a length of around 6 in/15 cm. The color and pattern varies but is usually a marbling

It should housed in a semi-humid terrarium with facilities for burrowing (leaf litter or orchid compost), and a water dish for bathing. Maintain temperate at around 81°F/27°C during the day, reduced to about

invertebrates such as grasshoppers, earthworms, and snails, but in truth they will, again, take just about anything. Beware of large specimens, for they can deliver excruciatingly painful bites.